Chris Mullin

Chris Mullin

Star Forward

Michael J. Sullivan

ENSLOW PUBLISHERS, INC.

44 Fadem Road	P.O. Box 38
Box 699	Aldershot
Springfield, N.J. 07081	Hants GU12 6BP
U.S.A.	U.K.

Library of Congress Cataloging-in-Publication Data
Sullivan, Michael John, 1960–
    Chris Mullin, star forward / Michael J. Sullivan.
       p. cm. — (Sports reports)
    Includes bibliographical references (p.) and index.
    ISBN 0-89490-486-8
    1. Mullin, Chris, 1963– —Juvenile literature. 2. Basketball players—United States—Biography—Juvenile literature. [1. Mullin, Chris, 1963– . 2. Basketball players.] I. Title. II. Series.
GV884. M85S85 1994
796.357'092—dc20
[B]
                                                   93-32727
                                                    CIP
                                                       AC

Printed in the United States of America

10 9 8 7 6 5 4 3 2

Photo Credits: Duomo, pp. 11, 20, 26, 90; Golden State Warriors, pp. 76, 94; Golden State Warriors, Photo by Sam Forencich, pp. 8, 17, 30, 55, 61, 66, 69, 72, 74, 78, 85; George Kalinsky, pp. 23, 38, 43, 52.
Cover Photo: Golden State Warriors, Photo by Sam Forencich

Contents

Chapter 1

Gold

The crowd was roaring. Golden State Warriors' superstar Chris Mullin was launching his jump shots against a great team, the Los Angeles Lakers, on April 17, 1991. In the fourth quarter, there was Chris driving past the Lakers for a beautiful spinning lay-up to give the Warriors a one-point lead. When the Lakers tried to lay back and stop Mullin's aggressive moves past them, Chris would take his world-famous jump shot . . . swish from the right corner and then swish from the left corner!

Mullin stole a pass, dribbled the ball near the foul line, jumped straight up into the air, and let go of the ball. Swish! The Warriors home crowd roared with delight. They had seen Mullin perform these same moves hundreds of times.

"There are times when Chris is just unstoppable," Los Angeles Lakers' General Manager Jerry West

*Mullin, alone under the boards, makes a lay-up as the
Los Angeles Lakers trail behind.*

said. "When he gets into that shooting groove, it doesn't matter where he is shooting from. It can be at the top of the circle, it could be deep in the corners . . . and the beautiful part of Chris's groove is the ball hits only the net. Let me correct myself . . . it can be beautiful if you are a Warrior fan, but it can be very upsetting if you have to play him."[1]

Chris hit two more jumpers in the closing minutes to help the Warriors to a much-needed win over the Lakers, 118–111. Chris led all scorers with 29 points. After the game, the ever modest Mullin credited his teammates with the win and refused to dwell on his performance. However, the Lakers were more than willing to praise him.

"When God made basketball," said Magic Johnson, "He said, 'Okay, I'm going to make a basketball player.' He just carved Chris Mullin out and said, 'This is a player.' And he is. I really respect Chris so much now. He's in that class. The class of guys who get my respect is tough to get into. I'm talking about guys, well, I hate playing against them. He's just a great basketball player."[2]

Magic was right. Mullin is a great basketball player. It appeared that not only players such as Magic were realizing that fact but the world as well. Recognition took place in the summer of 1991. The International Olympic Committee had decided the previous year that they would allow professional athletes to compete in the winter and summer games. So the cry around the United States was, "Let our basketball players play in Barcelona for the Gold." The United States Olympic Committee agreed, and the "Dream Team," comprised of the best NBA players, was formed. The ultimate sign of respect given to Mullin that summer was his selection by U.S. Olympic coach Chuck Daly to be part of the Dream Team.

"He is one of the best players in the world," Daly said at a press conference when the Dream Team was announced. "Chris Mullin deserves to be on this team because every part of his game is exceptional. He is a complete ballplayer, and he's a big part of our Olympic team. I look forward to working with him."[3]

However, before Mullin and Daly hooked up to challenge the world for the Gold Medal, Chris had to lead the Warriors to greater accomplishments in 1991–92. The Warriors had come off their best season in almost a decade, and expectations were high for 1992 around the Bay Area. Golden State got off to a flying start by winning their first four games, including a win over the Michael Jordan-led Bulls. Mullin scored a game-high 38 points and grabbed a team-high seven rebounds.

As part of the U.S. Olympic Basketball Team, Mullin was recognized as one of the world's greatest basketball players.

The Warriors put together several streaks of four or five games in a row. At one point in the season, Golden State won eight straight games in which Mullin led the team in scoring in five. Mullin was a picture of consistency, hitting for 30 points or more 24 times and scoring 29 points on five other occasions. For the fifth straight year, Chris led the Warriors in scoring (25.7) and was third in the NBA. He was also the second player in team history to average over 25 points a game in four straight seasons. Only the legendary Wilt Chamberlain has been able to accomplish that feat before.

"He's become such a great player where you are not even noticing the special things he does on the court because he's doing them so many times," said Blue Edwards, who plays for the Milwaukee Bucks. "What may be great for another player is just another day for Chris Mullin. He has done this so many times for so long that you kind of expect it from him. He's a player I don't look forward to playing against because he does so many things well."[4]

Mullin reached a milestone on December 17, when a jump shot from the right corner against the Minnesota Timberwolves gave him his 10,000th point in his NBA career. Chris also played in his fourth straight All-Star game and started for the Western

Conference for the second successive year. He also led the NBA for the second straight season in minutes played. It was becoming expected now that Chris Mullin would do what other players could not.

Chris became the first Warriors player to make the All-NBA First Team since Rick Barry did it in 1975–76. He also finished sixth in the Most Valuable Player balloting. His peers, the coaches and players of the NBA, realized now that Chris was one of the best players in the world. The great part of Mullin's personality was that he never yelled and screamed he was the best. "He just lets his playing do the talking," Edwards said. "He's always been like that. He's not a talker, but he's a heck of a player. There are other guys in the league who are always talking a great game, but Chris Mullin plays a great game."[5]

The Warriors hit their stride in 1991–92 with Mullin leading the way. They finished with a record of 55–27—their best regular season mark in 16 years. Even more impressive was that the franchise had its best road record, 24–17. Golden State was a highly explosive team on offense because of Mullin, and they led the NBA in scoring, averaging almost 119 points a game.

The Warriors had met all of the expectations that had been placed upon them before the season began. They had met the demands of the coaches and fans, but the NBA play-offs were another story. There was always the possibility of running into a hot team, and that would be dangerous for the Warriors. The first round was especially dangerous since the series was shorter in length. Instead of playing the usual four-out-of-seven games, the first round was a best three-out-of-five. One bad streak for the Warriors or one hot streak by their opponents, the Seattle Supersonics, and their great season would be wiped out.

The Supersonics were hot and lucky—both disastrous for the Warriors. Everything the Sonics shot went in, and everything the Warriors shot fell off the rim. Even on the Warriors' home court, the Sonics were terrific. Seattle won the first game, but the Warriors bounced back in the second game to even the series. However, the Sonics returned to Seattle with a chance to wrap up this short series at home. Seattle didn't disappoint its fans. The Sonics won game three by just a point and game four by just three to eliminate the Warriors from the play-offs.

The Warriors' loss was totally unexpected and very disappointing. The Warriors' fans, players, and coaches had felt so optimistic. But in one short series, their season was over. "Who would have thought that this would happen," said Rick Braun, who covers the NBA for the *Milwaukee Sentinel*. "It appeared that this would be their year. They had all of the right ingredients. They had one of the best players in the world in Chris Mullin. But that's the cruel part of the NBA playoffs. All the hard work and success you had in the previous 82 regular season games means nothing unless you can advance in the playoffs. And in the case of the Warriors, they just happened to run into a very hot team."[6]

The season was over for the Warriors, but a new one was beginning for Mullin—as part of the U.S. Olympic basketball Dream Team. Chris looked forward to playing with such great players as Magic Johnson, Michael Jordan, Patrick Ewing, Karl Malone, John Stockton, and David Robinson. Mullin was considered among the best in the world, and he was going to prove it.

The United States first had to qualify to play at the 1992 Summer Games in Barcelona. The Tournament of the Americas brought together several countries from the Western Hemisphere to compete for the right to play in the Olympics. The tournament was held at the Trail Blazers' home court in Portland, which gave the United States an immediate advantage. Mullin was simply fabulous. He averaged almost 15 points a game and was the only member of the Dream Team to score in double figures in all six games of the tournament. The United States easily qualified to play at the Summer Games.

"He has such great hands in all phases of the game," said teammate John Stockton, who plays for the Utah Jazz. "His shooting, his dribbling, his passing. I don't know if savvy is the right word. It's just his presence. I really don't think anybody else is as comfortable on the basketball court as he is."[7]

This was Mullin's second time at the Olympic Games. Chris's first time was in 1984 when he played for St. John's. That team was coached by Bobby Knight of Indiana. This time around Mullin was now established as one of the best players in the world, and he was being coached by Chuck Daly, who was used to dealing with professional athletes. The result was a more relaxed atmosphere for the U.S. basketball team. And it showed.

With so many great players on the team, it was rare that anyone played more than 25 minutes. But Mullin made the most of his time. The United States played Angola in the first round and easily won 116–48. Chris played 22 minutes and scored 11 points and had three assists. The next day the United States crushed Croatia, 103–70. Mullin scored four points but had six assists. It appeared that there wasn't anyone in the world who could stop the Dream Team.

Mullin talks with Olympic teammate John Stockton of the Utah Jazz.

"When you have players like Chris Mullin and Michael Jordan on the team, it's going to make it a little bit more easy to win the Gold Medal," said Magic Johnson. "Look at the players on this team. There isn't one player on this team that wouldn't be considered one of the best in the world."[8]

With Chris's outside shooting, the United States continued to win and win easily. They slammed Germany, 111–83. Mullin played 28 minutes and scored 13 points. It was in the next game against Brazil that Mullin started to "wow" the fans in Barcelona. Playing just 19 minutes, Mullin connected for three long-range bombs in the first half. First from deep in the right corner . . . swish! Mullin tried another from deep in the left corner . . . swish!

Chris hit three out of five tries from beyond the three-point line and also set up his teammates five times for baskets. Thanks to Mullin's performance, the United States battered Brazil, 127–83. The next game was probably going to be their toughest. The United States was going to play Spain on their home court in Barcelona. There was a loud crowd waiting to support their Spanish team, and they were going to make it rough on the U.S. team.

Fear not! When Spain would make a run, Mullin and his U.S. teammates answered with jumpers and lay-ups. Chris played 20 minutes and scored 14 points to help the United States to a 122–81 win. It was the toughest challenge the Dream Team had faced, and they made it look rather easy. The win over Spain advanced the United States to the quarterfinals. There they would face Puerto Rico, who had had some very good teams in the past. But Puerto Rico had never faced a team like this one.

Mullin hit several jumpers against Puerto Rico, including three more long-range bombs from beyond the three-point line. Playing just 22 minutes, Chris connected eight out of ten times. The only two shots he missed were from beyond the three-point line. Mullin scored 21 points and set up three teammates for easy baskets to help the United States defeat Puerto Rico, 115–77. Then the United States breezed past Lithuania, 127–76, to advance to the Gold Medal round against Croatia. However, it was not going to be easy. The last time the United States played Croatia, it was a close game until the second half. However, the U.S. players weren't going to let the Gold Medal slip away after all their hard work and effort.

Right from the opening tipoff, Mullin, Jordan, Johnson, and Ewing amazed the Barcelona crowd with their shooting and passing skills. They moved ahead quickly in the first half and were never caught. The United States easily defeated Croatia,

In the final match of the Olympics, the Dream Team defeated Croatia, 117–85

117–85. In his final Olympic game, Mullin scored 11 points in 17 minutes of play. He didn't miss a shot, and he also set up four teammates for baskets.

Chris averaged 13 points a game and shot a sizzling 62 percent from the floor, among the best of the Olympic athletes. He also finished the tournament as the United States second-leading scorer in Olympic competition with 196 points. Only Michael Jordan had done better. Mullin had done something few basketball players ever achieved—he was now a member of two Gold Medal teams!

FACT

When Chris helped lead the U.S. basketball team to the Gold Medal in 1992, he became one of six athletes in U.S. history to win two Gold Medals in basketball competition. The other five are:

Robert Kurland	1948 & 1952
William Hougland	1952 & 1956
Burdette Haldorson	1956 & 1960
Patrick Ewing	1984 & 1992
Michael Jordan	1984 & 1992

Chapter 2

Gym Rat

Christopher Paul Mullin was born in Brooklyn, New York, on July 30, 1963. In his preteen years, Chris was short, slow, and not too athletic. It wasn't long before he got the reputation as a gym rat, someone who is constantly shooting a basketball all day and night. However, people who saw him play when he was very young remember the special skill he had even when he was attending St. Thomas Aquinas grammar school in Brooklyn.

Tom Konchalski, publisher of *High School Basketball Illustrated,* first heard about him when Mullin was in the seventh grade. "Chris Mullin was small at that point in time, which became an advantage for him later in his career.

"Because he was small and slow and unathletic, his whole game was his ability to fake his opponent off his feet and get off his shot. That was

Chris Mullin learned his way around the basketball courts of Brooklyn, New York.

his special skill—his ability to use the 'ball fake.' And he had to have that skill when he was young because he was so small. He had to use deception in his game in order to have any chance of scoring."[1]

Chris also was fortunate to have a grammar school coach who cared enough to teach the basics of the game. It was in this area that Mullin moved ahead of most young players. His coach, Lou Piccola, taught Chris the basics of basketball and the proper time to try a ball fake.

"Chris is the smartest player in the city," said Piccola. "Some people question his quickness, but I'd much rather have him this smart than have him a little quicker."[2]

With Piccola's help, Chris Mullin's name started to be heard on the playgrounds of Brooklyn and Manhattan. "I heard the whispers coming from Brooklyn about this small, skinny kid," St. John's basketball coach Lou Carnesecca recalled. "That's the way things start. You do hear a lot of rumors during the course of the year about young players heading into high school. With Chris it was no different. But very few players live up to their playground reputations. And those that do, they are the special lot. Chris was in that special lot."[3]

The word around the Brooklyn playgrounds was that there was a skinny, Irish-looking kid making some noise on one of the nation's toughest basketball turfs. Because he was confident enough in himself to play against older and bigger players, Mullin became a better player. Chris let his playing do the talking on the courts of New York City.

"Chris was always good at moving without the ball," said Archbishop Molloy coach Jack Curran. "His drive and desire to get open was very much underestimated by his opponents. And when he did get the ball, he had that terrific ball fake. If you didn't go for the fake, Chris would drive around you."[4]

Chris's older brother, Rod, played for Brooklyn's Power Memorial High School. Rod, who later played for Siena College, graduated from Power Memorial in 1978. Naturally, Chris followed in his brother's footsteps and started his freshman year at Power in 1977. It was a logical choice for Chris since many of the best players from Brooklyn played for Power Memorial, including one of the world's greatest players ever—Lew Alcindor (who later changed his name to Kareem Abdul-Jabbar).

Mullin's freshman year at Power Memorial was a successful one. Even at the age of 14, Chris had the exceptional ability to move from side to side on the court. This ability enabled him to lose his defender and set up an easy jump shot for himself. Power won

Mullin's "ball fake" helped him compensate for his lack of speed.

the New York City Championship because of Chris's accurate shooting. Chris's sophomore year was no different than his first. Power Memorial won the Junior Varsity City Championship because of Chris's 25-points-per-game average.

"He was terrific those first two years of high school competition," *New York Post* writer Ken Wenthen said. "Those two Power Memorial teams were among the best you would see as far as court smarts. And it was because of Chris that this team played like a bunch of professionals. They knew what they were doing out there on the court, and these kids were just 14 and 15 years old!"[5]

Chris played in the Empire State Games the summer of 1979 and also attended the Five Star camp in Pittsburgh. This was considered one of the top basketball camps. There Chris played against some of the best high school players in the country and held his own.

"In fact, the talent was so good that a person by the name of Michael Jordan wasn't even invited because it was thought that he wasn't good enough," Konchalski said. "So, he [Mullin] held his own against the top players in the country. That's when schools like Duke and Virginia started recruiting Mullin. St. John's was always interested so Mullin's play certainly was beneficial for him and gave interest to the schools around the country."[6]

Chris's love affair with Power Memorial was interrupted in his junior year. Mullin missed playing with Brooklyn neighborhood pals Roger McCready (who later played for Boston College) and Mike O'Reilly, both of whom played for Xaverian High School. In addition, Lou Piccola, his grammar school coach, had moved to Xaverian. Chris, therefore, transferred from Power Memorial to rival Xaverian High School. However, because

FACT

Chris Mullin was named to the All-City CHSAA (Catholic High School Athletics Association) team by the *New York Post* for the 1980–81 season. Mullin averaged 30 points a game and 14 rebounds for Xaverian High School. The other four players to join Chris on the All-City CHSAA team were:

PLAYER	HIGH SCHOOL
Troy Truesdale	All Hallows
Mario Elie	Power Memorial
Dwayne Johnson	Mater Christi
Ernie Myers	Tolentine

his transfer was an athletic one, he was required to sit out one year. Chris played his first game for Xaverian in January 1981. One might think when a player sits out a year, he would be rusty. But not Chris Mullin. After all, he did have the best work habits in New York City.

A week after Chris returned from the one-year layoff, Xaverian had to play one of the top teams in New York City's tough Catholic league, Mater Christi of Queens. The star of that team was Dwayne Johnson, after Chris the next best player in New York City. Johnson scored 36 points, but Mullin bettered him with 37 points and also pulled down 10 rebounds to help Xaverian win in double overtime. It was Mullin's driving lay-up with two seconds left in the game that forced the first overtime.

Ken Wenthen, who was covering the game for the *New York Post*, attended the game with high school talent scout Tom Konchalski. Wenthen said, "It was one of the greatest one-on-one battles you would ever see. When Johnson would drive for a score, Mullin was down the other end doing his faking, slipping past a defender, and dropping in a jump shot. It was one of those city games you never forget."[7]

Interest in Chris peaked when he led Xaverian past Mount Vernon, 67–66, to win the New York State Championship. Mullin won the Most Valuable

An accurate jumpshot has been the key to Mullin's success.

Player award in the tournament after scoring 29 points and adding seven rebounds in the final. In his three seasons of high school ball, his team won three championship titles. He was also named to the McDonald's All-American team. Not bad for someone who played half a season in his senior year!

Mullin had a big decision to make—where to take his game for the next level of competition. Chris had received hundreds of scholarship offers from the top colleges and universities around the country. Among the schools who had caught Mullin's interest were Notre Dame, Duke, Virginia, and St. John's. A week after he led Xaverian to the New York State title, Chris told St. John's coach, Lou Carnesecca, that he was staying home to be close to his parents, Rod and Eileen. "I felt at home at St. John's," Mullin said back in 1981. "Plus, it was near my home, so I knew I could commute. Also, Coach Carnesecca never pressured me into going to St. John's. He wasn't all over me and pushing me to go. He made it known that no matter what happened my senior year, I would always have a scholarship if I wanted to go to St. John's."[8]

"Duke came in second for Chris, and they were really disappointed," Konchalski said.

FACT

Chris Mullin was one of the most heavily recruited players in the country as he was winding down his senior year at Xaverian High School in Brooklyn. It was a rare occasion back in the early 1980s that a New York City kid would stay home and play ball. Mullin stunned the college basketball world by choosing St. John's. The other schools he considered were: Duke University, University of Virginia, and University of Notre Dame.

"Coach Mike Kryzewski really liked Chris as a player and a kid. He took it upon himself to personally recruit Chris. I remember seeing Mike at the Wheelchair Classic in New York, and he had found out that day that Chris wasn't going to Duke but St. John's. He was really disappointed . . ."[9]

There was a sense of elation at St. John's and in New York City. For so many years, the great players had gone to colleges in other parts of the country. Now, one of their own was staying home to help revitalize college basketball in New York City. "I was so happy when we found out," said Lou Carnesecca, the beneficiary of Mullin's decision to play for St. John's. "I knew when he made his decision that we had something special there. He was going to give us a dimension and an excitement that this city hadn't seen in a long time."

Not since the days when the Knicks were the kings of the professional basketball world back in the late 1960s and early 1970s had there been such excitement. Mullin was just six when the Knicks won the NBA championship in the 1969–70 season. "Even if he didn't score, he adds 20 points to your team,"[10] Carnesecca said.

Chris Mullin was on top of the world, and he hadn't yet turned 18 years old. His ambition was to help lead the Redmen to the Final Four. He was willing to make whatever sacrifices that entailed. He was also looking forward to playing in Madison Square Garden in New York City, the home court of the Knicks and the place where St. John's played some of its home games. New York City was about to become Fun City again in the sport of basketball.

Chapter 3

St. John's

Playing in New York City can be a wonderful experience if you are a winner. When the New York Mets won the World Series in 1986, the city embraced and showered them with a celebration fit for royalty. But because of the size of the city's population, an estimated seven million citizens, people can be pretty rough on you very quickly if you don't win. St. John's basketball coach Lou Carnesecca knew that as Chris Mullin entered his first year as one of the Redmen in 1981.

The previous year St. John's had a number of excellent recruits, and a lot was expected of them. Besides signing Mullin, St. John's was also bringing into their program seven-foot center Bill Wennington, a Canadian native who had played his high school ball on Long Island, just 30 miles from the St. John's campus in Queens. With a sharpshooter like Mullin and a big center like

Wennington, there was an anticipation on the St. John's campus that something special could be happening over the next four years.

"I was certainly excited to have two players like that coming into the program," Carnesecca said. "To have a player like Chris who can do so many things was very important. He would help our outside shooting, enabling us to open up our inside scoring, and his ability to move and pass would only make our other players better. Did I expect him to fit in so perfectly so fast? No! But he did, right off the bat."[1] October 15 was the first day the National Collegiate Athletic Association (NCAA) allowed colleges and universities to begin varsity basketball practice. It wasn't long into the day before Carnesecca had his Redmen on the Alumni Hall floor taking jump shots and layups in preparation for the November start of the regular season. It also didn't take long before Carnesecca realized he had a player that could do things that the Redmen fans hadn't seen in a long time.

Mullin made an immediate impression on the coaching staff with his fluid style of getting himself open for a jumper or his ability to look at his teammate who had the ball and then cut to the basket and take the pass for an easy layup. Chris Mullin did this on the first day of practice. "It's like he had been here for 10 years," Carnesecca said after the first practice. "I'm usually pessimistic because I'm superstitious, but I was excited about this team."[2]

The excitement started to build when Mullin and the Redmen took the court for the first time for a regular season game. The occasion was the Joe Lapchick Memorial Tournament, named after one of St. John's greatest basketball coaches. There was also a rarity about to happen. Carnesecca was starting a freshman, something that the coach always tried to avoid because he didn't want to put any pressure on a first-year player. But Chris Mullin was no ordinary first-year player, and he showed his coach immediately. Mullin was simply . . . terrific!

In the first half of the game against Xavier University, Chris wowed the Alumni Hall crowd of 6,000 with jump shots from beyond 20 feet. First from deep in the right corner . . . swish! Again from in the right corner . . . swish! Each time the ball fell into Mullin's hands, everyone in Alumni Hall came to attention. When Mullin would softly release the ball, the crowd hushed as it spun toward the hoop. Swish! "Woooooow," the crowd roared.

The fans had certainly heard of Mullin, but to be able to make such an immediate impact was unheard of at St. John's. When Mullin wasn't "wowing" the crowd, he was helping his teammates to score. Chris threw a pass that whizzed past two Xavier players right into the hands of Redman David Russell who caught the ball and slammed home two points. "Wooow," the crowd roared as Mullin made the beautiful pass.

St. John's defeated Xavier of Ohio 75–55 to advance to the Lapchick Memorial final against the Fordham Rams, their local rival from the Bronx. "He's some player," said Mullin's teammate, David Russell. "It's going to be an interesting year, and it's going to be a lot of fun. I'm looking forward to this season."[3]

Most of the players from the Redmen knew the Fordham players because both teams recruited a lot of players from the New York area. St. John's expected a close and rough encounter with Fordham. Would Chris Mullin be able to handle the Rams' physical play? The Rams pushed, shoved, pressured, and talked to Mullin in the first half, trying to distract Chris's mind from playing basketball. Mullin simply paid no attention and moved around the court with the skill of a professional tightrope walker.

"Woooow," the crowd yelled when Mullin sank a jump shot. "Woooow," the crowd roared as Mullin, looking at his teammate Kevin Williams, instead

Chris Mullin receives the 1981 Joe Lapchick Memorial Tournament MVP Trophy from Barbara Lapchick, daughter of former basketball head coach, Joe Lapchick.

flipped a pass to a more open Bill Wennington on his right for a slam dunk. Up and down the court Mullin ran, not blinding the Rams with his speed, but managing to shake himself loose in the corners for jump shots. Swish! Swish! Swish!

The crowd continued to "oooh" and "ahhh" until Carnesecca thought it was time to give Chris a rest. St. John's had a 20-point lead, and Mullin had beautifully executed the Redmen team plan. The crowd at Alumni Hall gave Mullin a standing ovation as he left the court. Chris had scored 20 points for a total of 30 in his first two games at St. John's! How was Chris going to top it? Before Mullin had a chance to answer that question, the writers and broadcasters voted him the Most Valuable Player of the Joe Lapchick Memorial Tournament.

Mullin was quick to give credit to his teammates. "They got me the ball at the right times," Mullin said in the postgame press conference. "You have to give credit to my teammates because I wouldn't have won this award if it wasn't for them. I don't look at it as trying to top it. I just play it game to game. I am happy that I won the award but I'm more happy that we won the game."[4]

Chris Mullin would be repeating those same thoughts at the Holiday Festival in December at Madison Square Garden. It was the first time

Mullin had played in the Garden, the dream of every New York City youngster. Players such as former Knicks greats Willis Reed, Walt Frazier, and Bill Bradley had helped their team win two NBA championships in the late 1960s and early 1970s. Now, Chris Mullin was going to have a chance to play in the "Mecca of Basketball."

Mullin hardly blinked. He helped St. John's defeat Kansas, 76–75, and Villanova, 94–89, leading the Redmen to the Holiday Festival title. Chris was again selected by the writers and broadcasters as the Most Valuable Player of the tournament. "It's nice to be recognized by everybody, but it's more important that we won the game," Mullin said. "I'm glad we were fortunate because it was a tough game. You have to give credit to my teammates for helping me score. They deserve the credit. I was lucky."[5]

Mullin had already accomplished something that no one at St. John's had ever done as a freshman. He was named MVP of both the Lapchick Memorial Tournament and the Holiday Festival. New York City was just getting to know what Chris Mullin could do. The word was slipping out quietly. "Shhhh," said Carnesecca after he overheard a couple of reporters talking about the skills of Mullin. "Don't tell anybody just yet."[6]

Sorry, Lou. Word was getting out about Mullin and the Redmen. St. John's finished the season 21–9, ending their year by losing a heartbreaker to Alabama in the final seconds of an NCAA tournament game held at the Nassau Coliseum on Long Island, New York. The Redmen had three chances to win the game in the closing seconds but fell short. A disappointing end, but St. John's found out that they could compete with any college or university thanks to a player like Chris Mullin.

St. John's was a team on the rise. After a 21–9 season and all of their key players returning, St. John's was considered one of the favorites to win the Big East Conference for the 1982–83 season. Their first opponent, North Carolina, was ranked No. 1 in the country. What a way to start a season—against North Carolina in the Hall of Fame Tipoff Classic and on national TV! North Carolina was number one for a good reason. The Tar Heels featured Michael Jordan, James Worthy, and Sam Perkins.

The game was intense from the opening tipoff. St. John's would jump out to a five-point lead and North Carolina would come steaming back. Mullin quietly played his role for most of the first half, but in the second half Chris started to get rolling. He retrieved a loose ball near the North Carolina basket and moved near the mid-court line when he saw Worthy coming right at him. Mullin stopped as Worthy slipped, trying also to stop. Chris then drove past Worthy and moved to the left side of the foul line. Jordan came out toward Mullin, and Chris faked a jump shot. Jordan couldn't stop leaping in the air, and he flew right by Chris. Mullin then put up the jump shot . . . swish!

The game eventually went into overtime, and St. John's defeated the No. 1 team in the country, 78–74. For Mullin's 22-point effort, he was named co-MVP. "I hope we see more of them down the road," Jordan said afterward. "They're a great team, and this was a great game. And Mullin, he's pretty good, too."[7]

Mullin stayed "pretty good" the rest of the season. St. John's stayed in the Top Ten all season and won their first Big East Championship. St. John's defeated Boston College in the final game 85–77. Chris helped hoist Carnesecca high to let his coach enjoy the moment. But this was Chris's moment. The 19,500 people roared their approval when the announcement was made that Mullin had won the MVP. Chris's first goal had been achieved. He helped bring St. John's a Big East title. "I'm very happy we were able to win the tournament," Mullin said after the game. "It was an intense

St. John's began the 1982–83 season by defeating the number 1 team in the nation—North Carolina.

tournament with a lot of great teams. Now, I just hope we can go on and do some damage in the NCAA tournament."[8]

St. John's was seeded No. 1 in the Eastern Regional while North Carolina was seeded No. 2. Most fans and sportswriters were expecting a rematch of the first game of the season. What a great game that would be!

The Redmen played Rutgers University at Hartford, Connecticut, and bounced them from the tournament, 65–55. St. John's then flew to Syracuse to play Georgia in the third round. If St. John's got past Georgia, they would play North Carolina for the right to go to the Final Four. It appeared the Redmen would get their wish. St. John's moved out to a 10-point lead late in the first half. But two minutes before halftime, the lead had been sliced to four. Losing six points off their lead in an NCAA tournament game was significant. It appeared to deflate the St. John's players.

Georgia moved ahead early in the second half, and St. John's tried to play catch up the rest of the game. When St. John's got close, Vern Fleming of Georgia would slip through the Redmen defense with a lay-up. St. John's glorious season came to a stunning end, 70–67. There would be no rematch with North Carolina. After the game, the St. John's locker room was quiet. Mullin just stood at his locker, quietly putting on his shirt and tie. Very few words were spoken. Nobody had expected the season to end this way.

There was a look of amazement on Mullin's face as he left the Syracuse University locker room. He was disappointed, but he would be back. For Mullin's performances in 1982–83, he was named Big East Player of the Year. Chris was thankful for the award, but he had one goal to complete before he left St. John's: to make the Final Four. It was not going to be easy since seniors Kevin Williams, Bobby Kelly, Billy Goodwin, and David Russell were going to be leaving St. John's. Chris Mullin was not only going to have to provide St. John's with scoring but also with leadership on the court.

"He did both for us that year," Carnesecca said. "We asked him to do a lot of things in 1983–84, and he excelled in every part of it. Chris Mullin was the glue for us in his junior year."[9]

Chris had his best year statistically, averaging 23 points a game and almost five assists a contest. Mullin became the first St. John's player to average over 20 points per game since Glen Williams in 1976–77. He also averaged 39.6 minutes out of the usual 40 minutes of a game.

Thanks to Mullin's efforts, St. John's managed

to receive an NCAA bid despite an 18–11 record. Because they played in a tough conference like the Big East, the NCAA tournament committee deemed it proper to invite the Redmen. Unfortunately, this would be the shortest trip in the NCAA tournament for a St. John's team with Chris Mullin. In their first game, Terrance Stansbury hit a last-second 35-footer to spark Temple to a 65–63 win. Only moments before, Mullin had missed a foul shot that would have given St. John's the lead.

"It was a rough time," conceded Carnesecca when recalling the Temple loss. "I thought we had a great chance to advance. We did lose a lot of players from the previous season, but we had some good talent . . . and we had Chris. But I knew we were going to come back stronger. I knew that the next year we could go all the way to the Final Four. So the loss was disappointing, but I was certainly anxious about next year because we still had Chris."[10]

Mullin was named Co-Player of the Year in the Big East along with Georgetown's Patrick Ewing. Chris was also named a first-team All-American by United Press International and was picked for the Big East's first team. The awards were starting to pile up for Chris, but it never did impress him. "They are very nice because the recognition is flattering. I don't know if I will ever get used to it. I just try to play as hard as I can and help St. John's win."[11]

In Mullin's first three seasons as a Redman, St. John's did win. However, the best was yet to come for both Mullin and St. John's. But first, he was called upon by his country to help bring back the Gold Medal to the United States.

Chapter 4

Olympic Dream

Chris Mullin was about to face his toughest match so far. He had been invited to try out for the United States Olympic basketball team, and it would be his first face-to-face encounter with legendary Indiana coach Bobby Knight. It would take some time before Mullin would impress Knight. After all, Knight was one of the toughest coaches in the business. He sought perfection from his players and was never satisfied until he had received it. But Mullin was also someone who strove for perfection. He was more laid back than Knight, however, so it would be interesting to see how these two personalities got along.

"Bobby is the type of guy who will push and push and push," Carnesecca said. "But Chris is the type of player who will push and push and push.

When you have two forces pushing for the same goal, you will have successful results."[1]

Both Knight and Mullin were successful. Mullin made the Olympic team as a starter. Knight felt that Chris understood what he said and, more importantly, carried it out. "He's my kind of player," Knight said. "He listens. He works hard. He's got good instincts and creative skills. But, most of all, he wants to excel within the team concept. He's a definite winner."[2]

The competition at the Olympic Games was going to be tough, but the Soviets didn't show up. The Soviet Union decided to boycott the 1984 Summer Games in Los Angeles because the United States had boycotted the 1980 Summer Games to protest the Soviet invasion of Afghanistan.

Without the Soviets there, it appeared that the United States would have clear sailing to the Gold Medal. Mullin, playing with Knight's offensive system, averaged 12 points in eight contests. Not only did Chris impress Knight with his shooting and passing skills, but his hard-work ethic on defense also improved. "Every day he would push and push you until it got to the point where you thought you couldn't do it anymore," Mullin said. "But somehow Knight would get you to push yourself more."[3]

Mullin indeed did push himself more. Carnesecca recalled something that occurred when Mullin was about to head to the Olympic Games in Los Angeles. "I remembered, 'Oh my God, I forgot to call Mo and wish him luck for the Olympics.' So I felt kind of bad, and I thought maybe he's still around. So I passed the gym on my way home, and I hear the echoes of a ball being bounced. I walked in, and there was Chris! One hour from leaving on his plane and he's shooting around."[4]

It was obvious that Knight was pleased with Mullin's work ethic. "He did everything I asked him to do," Knight said. "It's not surprising that he has been successful because he works so hard."[5]

Mullin's winning attitude and outside shooting made himself, St. John's, his parents, and his country proud. The 15,000 people roared as each member of the U.S. basketball team received his Gold Medal. It's a moment that Chris will never forget. "It was a wonderful feeling to have the Gold Medal around my neck," recalled Mullin. "You dream all your life that something like that will happen to you. I always thought it was possible even when I was small and young. However, you have to be so fortunate to have it happen to you. To also play with so many great players and to perform before the whole world is such an honor. It's something I'll always treasure and cherish."[6]

Chris was tired, though. He had played almost every minute of St. John's regular season and had had to endure the stress and tension of Bobby Knight's practices and games. "He did look tired when he came back," Carnesecca said. "But we were so proud of him and what he accomplished. He was asked by one of the great coaches to push and push . . . and Chris pushed back harder. For that I was so proud of him."[7]

Mullin returned to the streets of Brooklyn with some gold. He was a hero now to the youngsters. Across the playgrounds of New York City, you could see many kids doing their Mullin moves. You could see the patented Mullin head fake, then the jump shot. "Mullin from 25 feet . . . swish!" the kids yelled from the city's hard courts.

Mullin was back home and happy—exhausted but happy. Now he was even more cautious about his fame because the nation knew of Chris Mullin and St. John's. Many preseason magazines picked the Redmen as No. 1 in the country. Chris and Georgetown center Patrick Ewing were on the cover of *Inside Sports* magazine. The media converged on the St. John's campus seeking information on Mullin and the Redmen basketball

When Mullin returned from the 1984 Summer Olympics, the St. John's sports information office was swamped with requests for signed photographs.

team. Everyday, the St. John's athletic office and sports information office would receive numerous requests and letters from across the country asking for autographed pictures of Chris Mullin. This shy, Brooklyn-born youngster was now living his dream. He was receiving more recognition than he had ever imagined possible. "I never saw anything like it," Carnesecca said. "I heard from people halfway across the world asking for tickets and autographs."[8]

St. John's was the best team in the country not only because of Mullin's sharpshooting skills but also because of the inside power game of center Bill Wennington. Newcomer Walter Berry added much-needed firepower from the inside, helping out Wennington with the rebounding chores. New York City was longing for a winner. It had been over 10 years since the Knicks had won a championship. The Redmen were about to make New Yorkers forget about the Knicks.

"Looking at our roster and who we have, I have to say this is the most talented team I've ever had," Carnesecca said, entering the 1984–85 season. "This team has great potential because we have so many offensive weapons. This team can do some great things."[9]

However, St. John's and Mullin started off

slowly. The Redmen struggled to win their first five games against weak competition and then lost to Niagara, 62–59. It was the jolt St. John's needed.

St. John's then won 19 straight games and captured the No. 1 ranking according to the Associated Press basketball poll. Once again, New Yorkers had fallen for St. John's. At that point Georgetown and Patrick Ewing came to town. The St. John's streak ended when Ewing scored 35 points. Georgetown also defeated St. John's in the final of the Big East Tournament, so the Redmen were sent to the Western Regional. Carnesecca said, "I was glad we were going because we needed a little break from people asking for tickets all the time. It was a wonderful stretch we had, but it was nice to go away and try to take care of business somewhere else."[10]

The Redmen were seeded No. 1 in the Western Regional by the NCAA committee, giving St. John's a good opportunity to advance. But they were seeded first because they had earned it. Their first-round opponent was Southern University at the Special Events Center in Salt Lake City, Utah, a peaceful place for St. John's to begin their road to the Final Four. However, nobody at St. John's had ever seen Southern play. Carnesecca needed help. He asked the citizens of New York through the newspaper reporters for videotapes of the Southern

Opponents were flying through the air when Mullin used his ball fake.

University team. Carnesecca received three the next day.

After struggling in the first half, Mullin's outside shooting heated up in the second half to help St. John's score an 83–59 win. The Redmen then held off Arkansas, 68–65, and Kentucky, 86–70, to advance to the final of the Western Regional. St. John's, who hadn't been to a Final Four since 1952, was one step away from making that magical trip again.

"We're just going to treat it like any other game," Mullin said before St. John's played North Carolina State at the McNichols Arena in Denver. "But I'd be lying to you if I said I wasn't excited. This is what I've been waiting for here at St. John's. I'm just thankful I can have a shot at it in my senior year. State is going to be a tough team."[11]

And for good reason, Mullin could have added. North Carolina State was coached by Jimmy Valvano, a man who guided his team to the NCAA championship in 1983. Valvano had been known to pull out miracles, but he made a big mistake in this game. Valvano instructed Spud Webb, just five feet six inches to guard the six-foot, six-inch Mullin. Valvano felt that Webb's quickness would be able to keep the ball out of Mullin's capable hands. However, Valvano should have realized that more than quickness was needed to stop a player like Chris Mullin, considered now one of the best college players in the country. Mullin had too much height and strength for the smaller Webb.

North Carolina State did stay close for most of the game, but when it counted at the end of the game, it was Mullin who rallied the Redmen with his shooting. The Wolfpack closed to within four points, and the St. John's fans began to get nervous. The ball was given to Mullin right at the foul line, and there was Webb, leaning into Mullin, eyeing the big orange ball. Mullin faked and used his six-foot, six-inch frame to muscle forward as Webb held his ground. Mullin jumped and shot . . . swish! And a foul on Webb! The St. John's fans roared. The guy they had relied on for so long was there in a crucial moment.

Mullin added some icing to the cake when he was given a pass by point guard Mike Moses near the foul line. Without looking and without catching the ball, Mullin deflected it to center Bill Wennington, standing right near the basket all alone! Dunk! St. John's fans were cheering and crying. Finally the Redmen were going to the Final Four. Carnesecca called on Mullin to come out of the game. The St. John's crowd roared, and the people

FACT

Chris Mullin was named the Player of the Year by the U.S. Basketball Writers Association in 1985. The balloting was conducted nationwide among the 1,200 members, and according to then Executive Secretary Joe Mitch the vote totals were the highest ever recorded. The runners up were:

1. Patrick Ewing

2. Keith Lee

3. Wayman Tisdale

4. Xavier McDaniel

5. Kenny Walker

6. Len Bias

7. Roy Tarpley

8. Dwayne Washington

9. Jon Koncak

from North Carolina State gave Mullin an appreciative round of applause.

Carnesecca gave Mullin a big hug. "Mo, Mo, we're going . . . we're going to the big party," Carnesecca said as he squeezed Chris hard. Mullin had a big, wide grin on his face. It was a picture captured by many of the newspapers around the country. "I know, I know," Mullin responded.[12]

The final buzzer sounded. The Redmen and their fans ran onto the court and hugged one another. St. John's was going to the Final Four, and to make matters even better . . . or worse . . . so were two other Big East schools, Georgetown and Villanova. For the first time in the history of the NCAA, three schools from the same conference were going to the Final Four. "That could hurt us because everybody knows how we play, and we have already played Georgetown three times this season," said a worried Carnesecca whose Redmen were to meet the Hoyas again in the first round at Lexington, Kentucky. "But we know them, too," Mullin said. "It's always a tough game when you play Georgetown because they play great defense."[13]

The Redmen practiced all week, but they already knew the style and players of Georgetown. All the practice in the world wasn't going to change anything for St. John's. They knew that this game was going to be their toughest of the year—and it was. Georgetown moved out to big leads on three occasions in the first half, and each time St. John's came storming back. But there was a noticeable difference in the Redmen offense—Mullin wasn't getting the ball. Everywhere Mullin moved, six-foot six-inch Georgetown guard Reggie Williams

FACT

Chris led St. John's to its all-time winningest record in 1985 with a 31–4 mark. That year St. John's also set the school's all-time consecutive win streak of 19 games. The 19 victims were:

1.UCLA	8.Boston College (twice)
2.Old Dominion	9.Syracuse (twice)
3.North Carolina State	10.Georgetown
4.Connecticut (twice)	11.Providence
5.Seton Hall (twice)	12.Columbia
6.Villanova (twice)	13.DePaul
7.Pittsburgh (twice)	

was right on top of Chris. And when Mullin got away from Williams, there was another Georgetown player immediately right beside Chris.

The Hoyas knew that if they could keep the ball away from Mullin, then the St. John's offense would have some problems. St. John's, down by 18 points in the second half, did make a heroic effort and moved to within four points with five minutes to go. But Mullin still could not get the ball, and Georgetown ended the St. John's season, 77–59. Mullin's college career was over.

"Give them all the credit in the world," Mullin said after the game. "They deserve the credit because they played a great game and great defense. This team has a lot to be proud of because of all their accomplishments."[14]

It was a sad way to end Mullin's fabulous career at St. John's. By his presence alone, he had revitalized interest in college basketball in New York City. Mullin led St. John's to the Final Four for the first time since 1952. Mullin was magic!

"He was one of those rare players who come along once in a lifetime," long-time St. John's Athletic Director Jack Kaiser said. "He brought a lot of excitement to our school and to our conference. You have to say he was one of St. John's greatest players ever, and that includes a lot of great company."[15]

Mullin finished his college career as St. John's all-time leading scorer.

Mullin left St. John's as its all-time leading scorer with 2,440 points. Chris was also named Big East Co-Player of the Year along with Patrick Ewing and received the John Wooden Award, given to the country's best player in honor of the former great UCLA coach. The awards were piling up for Chris, but he wasn't the type to sit around at home staring at all of his trophies. The day St. John's returned home from the Final Four, Mullin was in the St. John's gym working on his jump shot.

"What was that telling you?" Carnesecca said, shaking his head as he asked the question. "The season was over, but he was so dedicated and we were disappointed at how the season ended. He was out there working on his game. That's Chris . . . the ultimate gym rat to have played here at St. John's. There will never be another like him. He left us with a lot of great memories for St. John's."[16]

Carnesecca's then assistant coach Brian Mahoney went further in his praise: "Did we know he would take the city by storm like he did? No, of course, no one can predict the kind of success Chris had at St. John's. But it was a whole lot of fun watching him play and seeing the response of the St. John's fans and New York City. Every time he stepped out on the court, he was a man on a mission. He always played hard and for a purpose."[17]

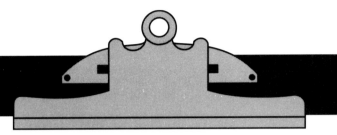

STATS

According to the St. John's Sports Information Department, Mullin holds individual scoring records for points in three classes: Freshmen (498), Sophomore (629), and Senior (694). In addition, Chris Mullin holds five career or individual Redmen records. They are:

Most points in a St. John's career	2,440
Highest free-throw percentage in a season	.904 (in 1983-84)
Highest career free-throw percentage	.847
Most free throws made in a career	682
Most free throws attempted in a career	805

There were more great memories ahead for Chris Mullin. The future for him was getting brighter. There was one more dream for Chris to realize—playing in the National Basketball Association. Now the shy kid from Brooklyn was going to have a chance to compete against players like Magic Johnson and Larry Bird. The biggest challenge still awaited Chris Mullin.

Chapter 5

The Pros

"The Golden State Warriors select . . . Chris Mullin from St. John's . . ." On that fateful June day in 1985, Mullin's professional career was born as the result of being selected by Golden State as the seventh player in the first round of the NBA draft. He was going to have to play professional basketball 3,000 miles away from his family and friends. Chris had hoped to stay at home or stay somewhere near home. After all, he had had great success playing in familiar surroundings.

"It's an adjustment I'm just going to have to make," Mullin said back in 1985. "It would have been nice to stay home and play in the NBA here, but I'm looking forward to becoming a Warrior and playing with and against some of the best players in the world."[1]

Though he was 3,000 miles from home, Mullin was happy to be playing in the National Basketball Association.

However, Mullin's NBA career was put on hold for a couple of months. Chris's agent, Bill Pollack, was not happy with the way contract negotiations were going. Since Mullin didn't have a contract, he sat out training camp in 1985 and missed the first six games of the season before signing a four-year contract on November 6, 1985. It was well worth the wait for Chris and the Warriors' fans.

That night the Warriors were home against the Seattle SuperSonics. The Golden State fans knew about Chris because of St. John's making the Final Four the year before. There was great anticipation over the presence of this hot-shot rookie. Mullin was called on by then coach John Bach to go into the game midway through the first quarter. The Golden State crowd cheered Mullin as he stepped onto the court for the first time as an NBA player.

The crowd got what it wanted. Mullin released his patented lefty jump shot from the foul line . . . swish! The crowd roared. They were warming up for many more moments like this. Mullin didn't play too long because it was his first game and he had missed training camp as the result of the contract dispute. However, Chris was inserted near the end of the game when the Warriors fell behind by two points with only 20 seconds left.

Time was running out for the Warriors. They needed at least two points to tie. Chris ran first to the left corner and then swung all the way over to the right corner. The ball came to him in a hurry. The clock was ticking toward 10 seconds. He didn't have much room to move in the right corner and had to watch his feet so he didn't step out of bounds. Mullin had to shoot now because time was running out. A SuperSonic leaped toward him, but Chris shot before he fell out of bounds.

Mullin had shot from beyond the three-point line! He was going for the win! The crowd, watching the ball as it left Mullin's hand, rose in unison. The big orange ball spun round and round toward the little metal hoop . . . swish! The crowd roared as if the Warriors had won the NBA championship. Mullin's three-pointer had saved Golden State from losing.

"That was something, wasn't it?" asked Mullin's teammate, Eric "Sleepy" Floyd. "You can't write a better ending for a rookie's first game. I'm looking forward to playing with him more. He's certainly a player that can help this team out."[2]

"I'm happy to just be playing," Mullin said after his first game. "You always dream that you are going to hit a shot like that at the end of the game,

In the final seconds of Mullin's first NBA appearance,
he scored a three-pointer that clinched the game for
the Warriors.

but I was fortunate enough to have it happen in my first pro game. It feels good to be playing again."[3]

Mullin played in 54 more games for the Warriors that season but missed the final 20 games because of a sore left heel. He registered some impressive numbers during his rookie season and helped the Warriors increase their total wins by eight, the second best improvement in the NBA that year. Chris finished second in the league in free throw percentage with a mark of .896, the second-best percentage for a rookie in NBA history.

Having missed the final 20 games of the season made Chris more determined the following year. He played in all 82 games of the 1986–87 season and improved his scoring average to 15.1. More importantly, the Warriors made the NBA play-offs and advanced past the Utah Jazz in the first round of the Western Conference bracket. The Warriors were then eliminated by the World Champion Los Angeles Lakers in five games. "I like some of the improvements I see in Chris's game," then head coach George Karl said. "He's more involved in the offensive flow, and he has so much potential. He has a great NBA career ahead of him."[4]

But every great player or great person has run into roadblocks somewhere down the road. Chris's roadblock was alcohol. It was catching up to Chris, and he had to do something about it. Mullin met the problem head on and voluntarily entered an alcohol rehabilitation program in early December of 1987. "He said to me that he just couldn't touch the stuff anymore," related his college coach, Lou Carnesecca. "It wasn't doing him any good, and it was affecting his everyday life. He faced the problem with such courage and strength."[5]

Mullin had plenty of support from family and friends, including his future wife, Liz. "That was very important because when you are down, you need people closest to you," Carnesecca said. "Chris had a lot of support from his friends, his family, and his agent [Bill Pollack]. I think that is what got him through."[6]

Chris Mullin returned not only a better player but also a happier person. He had met his roadblock with courage and had overcome his toughest challenge thus far in his young life. Mullin missed 22 games during the 1987–88 season, but the time he spent mending his problem was well worth it. "We're happy to have Chris back," said Karl. "We missed him, and he's an important part of this team."[7]

Chris averaged over 20 points a game for the first time in his NBA career and led the team in scoring with 1,213 points for the season. However,

After dealing with his alcohol problem, Mullin was happy to be back on the basketball court with the rest of the Warriors.

the Warriors weren't as fortunate. Coach George Karl resigned; a franchise record 21 players played for the team during the 1987–88 season; the Warriors had their second worst road record in history with a mark of 4–37; and Golden State finished fifth in the Pacific Division, a whopping 42 games out of first place.

Changes needed to be made at Golden State, and they were. General Manager Don Nelson became the head coach, and Chris Mullin's role in the offense became a more active one under Nelson. A new term emerged from the NBA when talking about Mullin's offensive role—"point-forward."

What Nelson planned to do was get the ball into Mullin's hands as much as possible. Since Chris had such great ability to score and pass, Nelson wanted to take advantage of his offensive skills. It worked! Chris played in all 82 regular season games during the 1988–89 season. He led the team in scoring with 26.5 points per game. It was good enough for fifth in the NBA! Chris was also second on the team in assists.

"When you have a player like Chris Mullin on your team, it's important that you utilize all of his skills because he has so many," Nelson said. "He's not only a great shooter but he's an exceptional passer, and I wanted to make sure that he had every

FACT

Chris Mullin is third on the all-time Warriors' list for making the All-NBA team. Chris has been selected four times. He trails Rick Barry who made six appearances and Wilt Chamberlain who made five.

Not known for his speed on the court, Mullin has been described as a "...slow, methodical, smart ballplayer."

opportunity to use his offensive skills. I'm happy that he has."[8]

Mullin was also extremely happy. He was improving from game to game and receiving the respect of his peers. Chris was named to play in the NBA All-Star game. It was another dream come true. "It's just a thrill to be here," Mullin said at the game. "You always dream that someday you would be recognized that you're among the best players in the league . . . and it's happened. I'm really fortunate for this to happen to me."[9]

It was a momentous occasion when Mullin played in the All-Star game. The previous year he had hit bottom when he went into rehab for an alcohol problem. He had not only hurdled his roadblock; he had won his race! Chris's parents, Rod and Eileen, were there along with several relatives and friends. "We were so proud of him," Carnesecca said. "He had come a long way, but he showed he had so much character. Mullin was among the best in the world at that point of his NBA career. And the best part of it was he was going to get even better."[10]

It was a terrific year for Chris. He had his best ever game in the NBA by scoring 47 points in a game against the Los Angeles Clippers. But it wasn't particularly satisfying for Mullin because the Warriors lost the game in overtime. However, Golden State did improve their regular season record by winning 23 more games than they had the previous year.

The Warriors returned to the play-offs, meeting the Utah Jazz in the first round. Mullin was simply fabulous. He averaged over 30 points and five assists a game to lead Golden State to a three-game sweep of the Jazz. "He is a master of the game's subtleties," teammate Tim Hardaway said. "He is a slow, methodical, smart ballplayer. You need to watch

Chris Mullin led the Warriors to the 1989 NBA playoffs.

him over time to appreciate the things he does out there. You have to watch how he uses his body, how strong he is. Every game he plays is a great game, as far as I'm concerned."[11]

In the next round, Mullin's great games were just not enough. The Warriors did win one game against the tough Phoenix Suns because of Chris's great outside shooting, but Golden State was eliminated from the NBA play-offs in five games. It was a year of many improvements both for the players and for the team. There was great anticipation for the 1989–90 season in the Bay Area of California.

Golden State set an all-time team attendance record by selling out all 41 home games, and Mullin led the team in scoring (25.1 points per game) and was second on the team in assists for the second straight year. But for some reason, the Warriors had difficulty maintaining consistency. Golden State would win five or six games in a row and then lose five or six straight. It was a season that confused both Mullin and head coach Don Nelson. When the Warriors were in New York that year to play the Knicks, Nelson and Mullin just couldn't quite explain to the local media what was going wrong. Both Mullin and Nelson did point out that the team wasn't consistent in its play.

But that was never the case for Mullin. For the

FACT

Chris Mullin has always wanted to play as often as he could. From January 29, 1988, to March 18, 1990, Chris played 190 games consecutively, a rarity in the NBA today. Chris is tenth on the all-time Warriors' list.

PLAYER	GAMES
Wilt Chamberlain	333
Phil Smith	321
Eric Floyd	306
Joe Graboski	288
Neil Johnston	286
Tim Hardaway	234
Rod Higgins	206
George T. Johnson	198
Joe Fulks	194
CHRIS MULLIN	190

Mullin's popularity helped renew interest in the Golden State Warriors, and soon all home games were sold out.

second straight year, Mullin was named to play in the NBA All-Star game. He was now considered by many sportswriters, sportscasters, and NBA players and coaches to be among the best players in the world. But the Warriors finished 37–45 and failed to make the play-offs.

"We have a lot to aim for," Mullin said right before the 1990–91 season started. "We have a lot of talent on this team and I think we can really improve over last season. I'm going to try my best and help this team win."[12]

Golden State did believe in Mullin. The Warriors won their first seven of nine games and maintained a consistent level of play during the entire season. The Golden State fans continued to support Mullin and his teammates. The Warriors once again sold out every home game, tying the franchise record for attendance in one season. The fans loved Mullin and rewarded him by voting him a starting spot on the Western Conference squad for the 1991 NBA All-Star game in Charlotte.

"It's always an honor to be selected for the All-Star game," Mullin said in Charlotte. "But to have the chance to start in it is something you always dream of but never think is going to happen. I'm lucky enough to have it happen."[13]

Lucky? Perhaps. But Mullin deserved to be

there and proved it by scoring 13 points in the game. Mullin was also a team player and wanted to show that in the All-Star game. Chris added two assists, including a beautiful touch pass to set up Magic Johnson for an easy basket. Mullin's skills were especially appreciated by Johnson. "You can't help but like Chris Mullin," Johnson said later of his teammate. "He's everything you want in a basketball player and in a teammate."[14]

The Warriors continued their winning ways during the early part of 1991 and claimed their best regular season record in nine years with a 44–38 mark. For the third straight season, Chris led Golden State in scoring with 25.7 points per game and was second on the team in total assists.

"He did everything for us," Coach Nelson said. "You couldn't ask for more from a player. He's one terrific player. He gets to guys. He motivates them. And they adopt his work habits."[15]

The Warriors returned to the NBA play-offs to face the Midwest champions, the San Antonio Spurs with one of the NBA's top centers, David Robinson. It was going to be a difficult task indeed. Golden State lost the first game at San Antonio but managed to go home with a win by defeating the Spurs in the second game.

This first-round match-up was a best 3-out-of-5,

FACT

Chris Mullin has always been a terrific free-throw shooter, and some of his best shooting has been in the play-offs. Mullin holds the Warriors' record for most free throws made in a play-off game with 16. Chris also holds a piece of the Warriors' record for most free throws attempted in a play-off game with 19. Rick Barry did it in 1967.

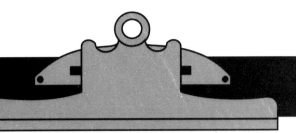

STATS

Chris Mullin has always been known as a clutch performer, and his play with the Warriors is no different. According to the *Golden State Warriors Media Guide*, Mullin is listed in the top ten career play-off leaders in 10 different categories. They are:

CATEGORY	RECORD	RANK
Total points	609	6
Scoring average	20.3	7
Blocked shots	27	6
Steals	43	5
FGA	455	10
FGM	233	9
FG percentage	.512	4
3-point FGA	37	4
3-point FGM	17	3
FT percentage	.857	5

so if the Warriors won the next two on their home court, they would advance to the second round. Game three was a tough one. The Spurs and Warriors exchanged leads several times in the first and second halves. But the Warriors had something the Spurs didn't—Chris Mullin.

Mullin hit four jumpers in the fourth quarter under pressure situations to help the Warriors go into Game 4 with a 2–1 lead and a chance to wrap up the series. Mullin and the Warriors played a perfect game. Golden State moved into the second round of the play-offs with a 110–97 win over the favored Spurs.

The next challenge for Mullin and the Warriors was the legendary Los Angeles Lakers, who still had Magic Johnson. The Warriors had never been too successful at Los Angeles, and they had to play the Lakers there for the first two games. After losing the first game, the Warriors topped the Lakers in Game 2 to return home with the series tied, 1–1. The Warriors' crowd was loud and supportive throughout Game 3. The second half was an exhibition of brilliant basketball. First it was Magic Johnson, scoring and setting up his teammates. Then it was Chris Mullin, topping Johnson's every move. Unfortunately for Mullin and Golden State, the Lakers had too many good players and slipped past the Warriors in Game 3 with a 115–112 win.

The Lakers also won Game 4 at Golden State and returned to Los Angeles with a 3–1 lead and a chance to clinch the series. The Warriors and Mullin didn't quit. They battled Los Angeles into overtime before losing, 124–119. The season had ended, but the optimism for next year began as the Warriors got off the plane from Los Angeles.

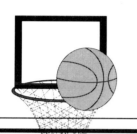

Chapter 6

A Marked Man

A little man bounced around in the middle of the ballroom floor. His scratchy voice with the New York accent greeted some familiar and not-so-familiar faces. He moved around the hotel floor like a politician shaking hands while working the subways during rush hour. Smiles and backslaps were the only gestures appropriate for this occasion.

This little man was Lou Carnesecca, former basketball coach for the Redmen of St. John's University. Carnesecca was not unlike the other 200 people gathered for this special event. They were present to honor St. John's greatest player ever—NBA All-Star Chris Mullin—at a fund raiser for St. John's alumni on the West Coast in September of 1992.

Mullin arrived with his wife Liz and son Sean. "Mo, Mo," Carnesecca cried, using his nickname for Mullin. "How are you doing? It's great to see you and your family."[1]

"Great to see you, Coach. How are you?" Mullin said as he put down Sean's diaper bag. "What's new?"[2]

Their conversation lasted about 10 minutes as the two exchanged many words of encouragement. Then Mullin reached down into the diaper bag. It was one of many new rituals that Chris had learned since becoming a new daddy.

"Hey, Coach, look what I dropped into the diaper bag,"[3] Mullin said. Chris pulled out a diaper

Many people have described Chris Mullin as a very special giving person. He has been involved in raising money for causes like the United Way, and the American Cancer Society.

that contained a shiny object. Grinning brightly, Chris held up the gold-painted medal, his prize for helping the United States Dream Team capture the Gold Medal at the 1992 Summer Olympics in Barcelona.

"You know he is a very special person, someone who is very kind," Carnesecca recalled later. "He cares about the people who are close to him. He has always had a kind word to say to me and my family. He never forgets the people here at St. John's. He always comes back to see the coaches here at St. John's and say hello," Carnesecca said. "He's developed into an even better player in the pros than he was at St. John's. But more importantly, it's great to see what a great father and husband he is. He has a lot of good in him."[4]

Mullin does have a lot of kindness in him. Chris supports the American Cancer Society and the Leukemia Society of America with contributions and charity work. Mullin also had other things on his mind. He became a father in June 1992 when his wife Liz gave birth to a son they named Sean. Life was good for Chris Mullin at this moment. He was never one for taking anyone or anything for granted. He wanted to give something back to the community that had given him so much, so he formed the United Way's Chris Mullin Fund for Families. It was designed to help the needy families of the Bay Area.

"I'm very happy and grateful," Mullin says. "I remember when things weren't like this. It's almost like I want to bottle this feeling because I know things can be different. And they were different. So now, yeah, I'm probably the most happy I've ever been."[5]

Lou Carnesecca remembers when things were different for Chris in 1991. At that time Chris was faced with a terrible family crisis.

"One of the most touching moments I've ever experienced was when we had a sports dinner at St. John's," Carnesecca recalled. "He (Mullin) looked at his dad during his speech and Chris's dad was sick. Chris was choked up and all he could say was 'Dad, I love you.'

"I was supposed to speak next and I couldn't speak," Carnesecca added. "I just couldn't speak . . . I just couldn't get up. You could see that he loved him so much by saying 'Dad, I love you.' It was one of the most touching moments."[6]

St. John's Public Relations Director Martin Healy agreed with Carnesecca. "It was one of the most human and emotional sentences I've heard spoken at a sports dinner," Healy said. "There was just a hush over the crowd when he said it. There wasn't a dry eye in the house. I think it showed that there was more to Chris Mullin than hitting a jump shot to win a game."[7]

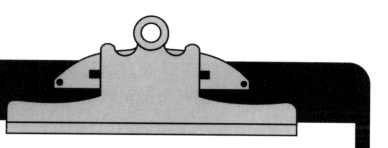

STATS

Chris Mullin does hold the all-time record for points scored for St. John's, but he played before the college game added the three-point line. However, Chris has more than made up for that in the NBA. Chris holds the Warriors' record for most FG's made without a miss. Mullin accomplished that feat with 11 against the Miami Heat on December 1, 1990. His other three-point records for the Warriors are:

CATEGORY	RECORD
Most 3-pt FG's made in an individual play-off game	4
Most 3-pt FG's made in an individual play-off game without a miss	4
Most 3-pt FG's made in a regular season game	6

A few months after the dinner an article appeared in a major magazine. It contained some unkind words about Mullin's father, who had died from cancer in 1991. Chris did not respond to the negative article with bitterness or anger. Mullin showed he could be more kind than the author of the article.

"Some guys took a shot, but when you think about it, did it make the story any better," Carnesecca questioned. "Chris was better than that. It hurt him that it was written, but he remained positive about life and his family."[8]

Then he had to get himself ready for the 1992–93 season. Though the Warriors had had a successful regular season last year, there were a lot of disappointed people in the Bay Area after the Warriors lost in the play-offs. The new season was a rough one both for Golden State and Mullin. He was again the Warriors' most consistent player, but they could never get a long winning streak going. Golden State lost one of its top players, Billy Owens, to an injury early in the season. In fact, the Warriors' top four scorers from last season played just three minutes together all season long.

The Warriors struggled to stay in play-off contention, and Mullin continued to lead the assault by averaging over 25 points a game. He had avoided the injury jinx, but in late January he hurt his thumb

After his success at the Olympic Games in Barcelona, Mullin was disappointed with Golden State's 1992–93 season. A thumb injury caused him to miss most of the season.

against the Los Angeles Clippers. Chris had some swelling in his right thumb. A torn ligament was suspected. It was obvious that it was bothering Mullin. However, on February 2, 1993, Chris scored 17 points against the Cavaliers in Cleveland. It was the 300th straight game in which Chris had scored 10 or more points. Only Michael Jordan, with 542 games at that point, had a longer streak.

After playing against the Knicks in New York on February 4, Mullin said, "It's not excruciating pain, but I don't think it helps handling the ball, catching the ball. I'd rather play without tape, but they tape me because they don't want me to hurt it worse."

It got worse. Mullin didn't play in the Warriors' next game against the Celtics in Boston on February 7. He underwent surgery on his thumb and was forced to sit out the rest of the season as the league's fourth-leading scorer (26.5 points a game). But despite the season's disappointing end, Mullin kept everything in perspective.

"The worst day in our lives is not too bad," he said. "We're playing ball. You lose games. You try to go out there and win. But if you don't, you keep on plugging away."[9]

Mullin has grown to six feet, seven inches and 215 pounds since he left St. John's University in 1985. His arms are bigger, his chest has expanded, and he has a capability to play the full 48 minutes in an NBA game. This part of Mullin's game is certainly appreciated by many of his opponents. "The guy never seems to tire out," said Blue Edwards of the Milwaukee Bucks. "You think you are able to stop him late in the game because he's been on the court the whole night. But, you can't! Mullin will just keep on coming at you whether it's the first minute of the game or in triple overtime."[10]

Mullin has become one of the world's best players through hard work and dedication. Chris has averaged over 20 points a game for six straight seasons as a Warrior. He scored his 10,000th career point during the 1991–92 season and became the first Warrior to start in an NBA All-Star game (1991) since the legendary Rick Barry in 1978.

"He may be the smartest player in the league," Detroit Pistons' guard Joe Dumars said. "I just love the way he plays the game. He's never in a hurry and always in control of what he's doing."[11]

Mullin has produced some historic numbers, too. Chris became the third player in Warriors' history to total 2,000 points, 400 rebounds, and 400 assists in the same season. Among the great players Mullin joined on the list—Wilt Chamberlain and Rick Barry!

"He has turned into one of the world's best

STATS

Despite Chris's relatively short NBA career, he is now placed in 16 regular season individual categories on the Warriors' top ten all-time list.

CATEGORY	RECORD	RANK
Total points	12,727	5
Scoring average	22.5	6
Assists	2,171	8
Steals	994	1
Blocked shots	341	7
Minutes played	20,287	6
Offensive rebounds	731	7
Defensive rebounds	1,841	6
FTA	3,154	6
FTM	2,741	6
FT percentage	.869	2
FGA	9,339	7
FGM	4,827	7
FG percentage	.517	7
3-pointers made	332	2
3-pointers attempted	962	2

One of the best players in the history of the Golden State
Warriors, Chris Mullin will continue to lead his teammates
toward the ultimate goal—an NBA championship.

all-around players," said high school super scout Tom Konchalski, who has seen Mullin play since Chris was 12 years old. "Every part of his game has developed since he was just a baby. And he has gotten better with every level he has reached. That is a sign of a great player. But in a way, it's not that surprising. Chris has always worked hard. He's always been dedicated to the game of basketball, and it shows in his continuing improvement. Chris Mullin can be proud of his accomplishments because he is one of the world's best players."[12]

Notes by Chapter

Chapter 1

1. Jerry West, Interview by author, December 6, 1989.

2. *Golden State Warriors Media Guide*, October 1991, p. 50.

3. NBC-TV, New York City, July 7, 1991.

4. Blue Edwards, interview by Rick Braun, Milwaukee, Wisconsin, January 3, 1993.

5. Ibid.

6. Rick Braun, Interview by author, January 25, 1993.

7. John Stockton, interview by Rick Braun, Milwaukee, Wisconsin, January 3, 1993.

8. Magic Johnson, interview by Rick Braun, Milwaukee, Wisconsin, January 3, 1993.

Chapter 2

1. Tom Konchalski, Interview by author, December 15, 1992.

2. Ken Wenthen, *New York Post*, February 1, 1981, p. 92.

3. Lou Carnesecca, Interview by author, November 17, 1992.

4. Jack Curran, Interview by author, March 30, 1990.

5. Ken Wenthen, Interview by author, December 12, 1992.

6. Ibid.

7. Tom Konchalski, Interview by author, December 15, 1992.

8. Chris Mullin, Interview by author, October 15, 1981.

9. Tom Konchalski, Interview by author.

10. Lou Carnesecca, Interview by author, November 17, 1992.

Chapter 3

1. Lou Carnesecca, Interview by author, November 26, 1992.

2. Lou Carnesecca, Interview by author, October 15, 1981.

3. David Russell, Interview by author, November 28, 1981.

4. Chris Mullin, Interview by author, November 29, 1981.

5. Chris Mullin, Interview by author, December 29, 1981.

6. Lou Carnesecca, Interview by author, November 30, 1981.

7. Michael Jordan, Interview by author, November 20, 1982.

8. Chris Mullin, Interview by author, March 12, 1983.

9. Lou Carnesecca, Interview by author, November 26, 1992.

10. Lou Carnesecca, Interview by author, November 26, 1992.

11. Chris Mullin, Interview by author, October 15, 1992.

Chapter 4

1. Lou Carnesecca, Interview by author, November 26, 1992.

2. Richard O'Connor, "Chris Mullin, Is He Another Bradley," *New York Sports* (February–March 1985), p. 41.

3. Ibid.

4. Lou Carnesecca, Interview by author, November 26, 1992.

5. Bobby Knight, Interview by author, July 20, 1989.

6. Chris Mullin, Interview by author, October 15, 1984.

7. Lou Carnesecca, Interview by author, November 26, 1992.

8. Ibid.

9. Ibid.

10. Ibid.

11. St. John's University Sports Information Office, March 15, 1985.

12. St. John's University Sports Information Office, March 25, 1985.

13. Lou Carnesecca, Interview by author, March 27, 1985.

14. St. John's University Sports Information Office, March 30, 1985.

15. Jack Kaiser, Interview by author, June 30, 1991.

16. Lou Carnesecca, Interview by author, November 26, 1992.

17. Ibid.

Chapter 5

1. Chris Mullin, Interview by author, June 30, 1985.

2. Eric Floyd, Interview by Rick Braun, Milwaukee, Wisconsin, November 6, 1992.

3. Chris Mullin, Interview by Rick Braun, Milwaukee, Wisconsin, November 6, 1992.

4. George Karl, Interview by Rick Braun, Milwaukee, Wisconsin, November 6, 1992.

5. Lou Carnesecca, Interview by author, November 26, 1992.

6. Ibid.

7. George Karl, Interview by Rick Braun, Milwaukee, Wisconsin, November 6, 1992.

8. Don Nelson, Interview by author, December 4, 1989.

9. Chris Mullin, Interview by Rick Braun, Milwaukee, Wisconsin, November 6, 1992.

10. Lou Carnesecca, Interview by author, November 6, 1992.

11. *Golden State Warriors Media Guide*, October 1992, p. 50.

12. Chris Mullin, Interview by Rick Braun, Milwaukee, Wisconsin, November 6, 1992.

13. Chris Mullin, Interview by Rick Braun, Milwaukee, Wisconsin, November 6, 1992.

14. *Golden State Warriors Media Guide*, p. 51.

15. Ibid.

Chapter 6

1. Lou Carnesecca, Interview by author, November 26, 1992.

2. Ibid.

3. Ibid.

4. Ibid.

5. Ibid.

6. Ibid

7. Martin Healy, Interview by author, December 12, 1992.

8. Lou Carnesecca, Interview by author, November 26, 1992.

9. Joe Donnelly, *New York Newsday*. February 5, 1993, p. 158.

10. Blue Edwards, Interview by Rick Braun, Milwaukee, Wisconsin, October 17, 1992.

11. *Golden State Warriors Media Guide*, p. 49.

12. Tom Konchalski, Interview by author, December 28, 1992.

Career Statistics

YEAR	TEAM	G	FG%	REB	AST	STL	BLK	PTS	AVG
1985-86	Warriors	55	.463	115	105	70	23	768	14.0
1986-87	Warriors	82	.514	181	261	98	36	1,242	15.1
1987-88	Warriors	60	.508	205	290	113	32	1,213	20.5
1988-89	Warriors	82	.509	483	415	176	39	2,176	26.5
1989-90	Warriors	78	.536	463	319	123	45	1,956	25.1
1990-91	Warriors	82	.536	443	329	173	63	2,107	25.7
1991-92	Warriors	81	.524	450	286	173	62	2,074	25.6
1992-93	Warriors	46	.510	232	166	68	41	1,191	25.9
1993-94	Warriors	62	.472	345	315	107	53	1,040	16.8
1994-95	Warriors	25	.489	115	125	38	19	476	19.0
1995-96	Warriors	55	.499	159	194	75	32	734	13.3
TOTALS		708	.512	3,191	2,805	1,214	445	14,977	21.2

Where to Write
Chris Mullin

Mr. Chris Mullin
c/o Golden State Warriors
Oakland Coliseum Arena
7000 Coliseum Arena
Oakland, CA 94621

Index

New York State Championship, 29
Niagara University, 54
North Carolina State, 56–59

O

Old Dominion University, 59
Olympics, 9–10, 15–16, 18–19, 48–50, 86, 90
O'Reilly, Mike, 28
Owens, Billy, 89

P

Pacific Division, 73
Perkins, Sam, 41
Phoenix Suns, 77
Piccola, Lou, 24, 28
Pittsburgh, University of, 59
point-forward, 73
Pollack, Bill, 67, 71
Portland Trail Blazers, 15
Power Memorial High School, 25, 27–28
Providence University, 59

R

Reed, Willis, 40
Robinson, David, 15, 80
Russell, David, 37, 45
Rutgers University, 44

S

St. John's University, 16, 24, 27, 31–37, 39–41, 44–47, 50, 51, 53–54, 56–60, 63, 67, 84, 86–87, 91
St. Thomas Aquinas Grammar School, 22
San Antonio Spurs, 80, 82
Seattle Supersonics, 14, 67–68
Seton Hall, 59
Siena College, 25
Smith, Phil, 77
Southern University, 54

Stansbury, Terrance, 46
Stockton, John, 15, 16
Syracuse University, 45, 59

T

Tarpley, Roy, 58
Temple University, 46
Tisdale, Wayman, 58
Tournament of the Americas, 15

U

United Press International (UPI), 46
United Way, 85
University of California at Los Angeles (UCLA), 59
U.S. Basketball Writers Association (USBWA), 58
Utah Jazz, 16, 17, 70, 76

V

Valvano, Jimmy, 56
Villanova University, 58–59
Virginia, University of, 27, 31

W

Walker, Kenny, 58
Washington, Dwayne, 58
Webb, Spud, 56–57
Wennington, Bill, 34–35, 39, 53, 57
Wenthen, Ken, 27, 29
West, Jerry, 7, 9
Western Conference, 12–13, 70, 79
Western Regional, 54, 56
Wheelchair Classic, 32
Williams, Glen, 45
Williams, Kevin, 37, 45
Williams, Reggie, 59
Worthy, James, 41–42

X

Xaverian High School, 28–29, 31
Xavier University, 36–37